Map

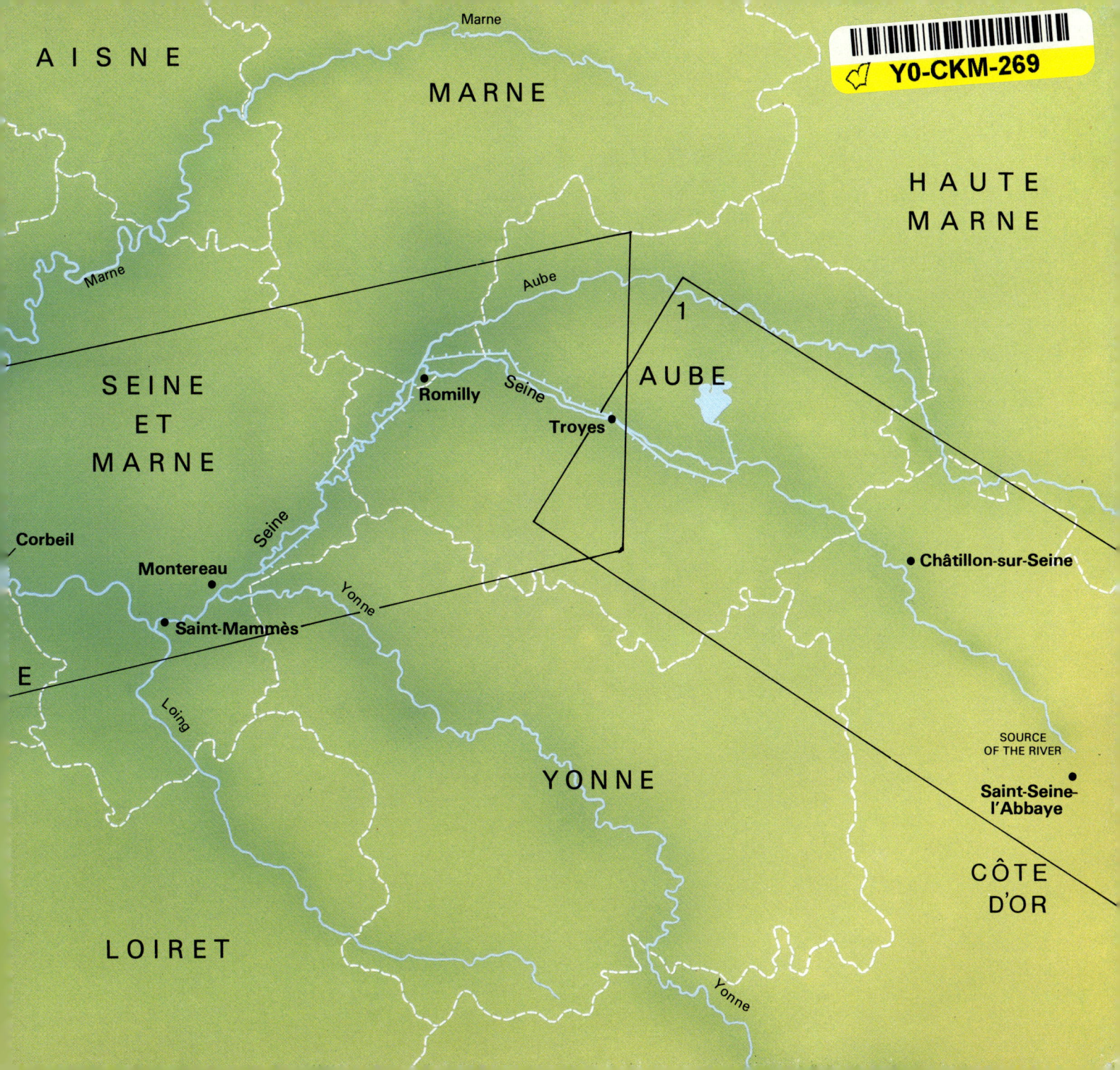

AISNE · **MARNE** · **HAUTE MARNE**

SEINE ET MARNE · **AUBE** · **1**

Marne · Aube · Seine

Romilly · Troyes

Corbeil · Montereau · Saint-Mammès

Seine · Yonne · Loing

YONNE · Châtillon-sur-Seine

SOURCE OF THE RIVER
Saint-Seine-l'Abbaye

LOIRET · **CÔTE D'OR**

Y0-CKM-269

A journey down the Seine

The Seine is the most famous river in France. It begins its life in a little wooded valley in Burgundy. It flows through Paris and then on to the sea past the industrial centres of Rouen and Le Havre.

In this book we shall take a journey down the Seine from its source to its mouth in the English Channel. We shall look at its people, its cities and its industries and discover why so many artists have felt moved to paint it.

River Journeys

A journey down the Seine

Laurie Bolwell

Wayland

River Journeys

A journey up the Amazon
A journey down the Danube
A journey down the Ganges
A journey down the Mississippi
A journey up the Nile
A journey down the Rhine
A journey down the Seine
A journey down the Thames

This book is based on The Seine, *in Wayland's 'Rivers of the World' series, by C. A. R. Hills.*

First published in 1985 by
Wayland (Publishers) Ltd
49 Lansdowne Place, Hove
East Sussex BN3 1HF, England

© Copyright 1985 Wayland (Publishers) Ltd

ISBN 0 85078 534 0

Filmset by
Latimer Trend & Company Ltd, Plymouth
Printed in Italy by
G. Canale & C.S.p.A., Turin
Bound in the UK by The Pitman Press, Bath

Contents

The River Seine   8

From the Source to Troyes   12

On the Outskirts of Paris   18

The Seine in Paris   22

The Suburbs of Paris   34

The Seine in Normandy   44

The Seine Estuary   58

Glossary   64

Index   66

The River Seine

Here is one of the most famous sights on the River Seine.
It is the cathedral of Notre Dame in Paris.
Notre Dame stands on an island in the centre of the city.
You can see a large working **barge** passing by.

The Seine is not a very long
river, only 780 km (485 miles).
But it flows through the heart
of France.
It begins in quiet woods in
Burgundy.
Then it flows gently on to Paris
and on to the sea past
the industrial towns of
Rouen and Mantes.
There are many quiet spots
where people fish and swim.

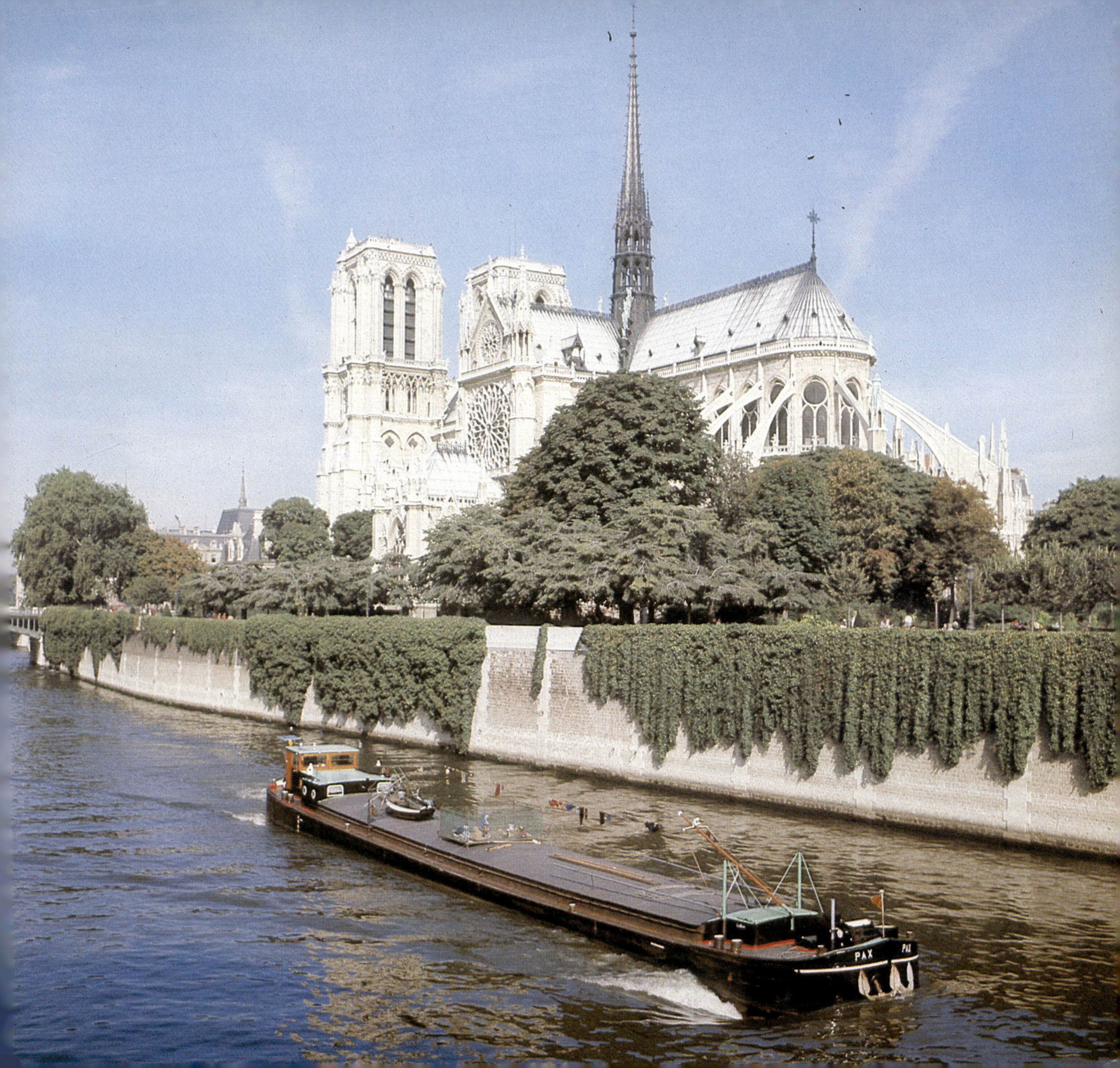
PAX

This is a famous painting of the Seine by the artist Seurat.
How can you tell that it was painted some time ago?
It shows a hot sunny day with people enjoying the river.
In the background you can see factories.

There are still many artists in Paris and you can often see them working beside the River Seine.
This man is painting with oils.
Can you see what he is painting?

The Seine is a calm river which flows smoothly.
It does not have to fall a great distance to the sea.
Its source is only 471 metres (1,545 feet) above sea level.
So there are no great waterfalls.
Nor are there dangerous floods.

Because it is calm it is a safe river for traffic.
The River Seine is very busy from Paris to the sea.
There are many working barges.

From the Source to Troyes

The Seine rises in Burgundy.
A path in the woods leads to a pool where the Seine begins.
Beside the pool is a statue of the river goddess, Sequana.

This is the statue of the goddess Sequana.

From the pool the tiny stream begins its journey to the sea. Here it is narrow enough for a child to jump across.
It may even dry up in summer.

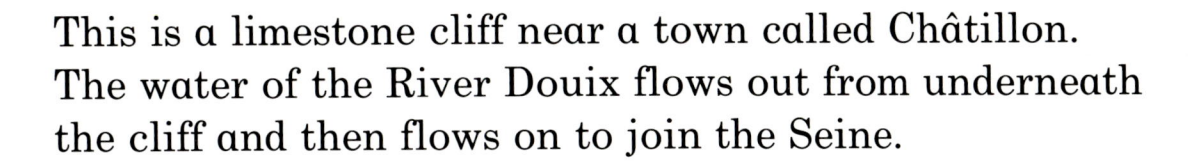

This is a limestone cliff near a town called Châtillon. The water of the River Douix flows out from underneath the cliff and then flows on to join the Seine.

Châtillon is the first town
you reach on the river.
Here is a picture of the
church and some old houses.
Many houses in the town are new.
Many old buildings were
destroyed in the Second World
War when the town was bombed.

People have lived in this area
for thousands of years.
The grave of a princess who
lived 2,500 years ago has
been found.
She had been buried with her
jewellery and treasure.
This part of the Seine was
then a rich trade route.

This is a village scene
in Burgundy.
The water of the Seine is
clear and pure here.
So the women do their
washing in it.
This is the village laundry.
The children can swim while
their mothers work.

After Châtillon the Seine
leaves Burgundy.
It flows into Champagne.

Champagne is a **province** of France famous for its wine.
But most of the vineyards are well away from the Seine.
In this region the Seine is still a very small river.
Even the tiniest barges cannot get this far up the river.

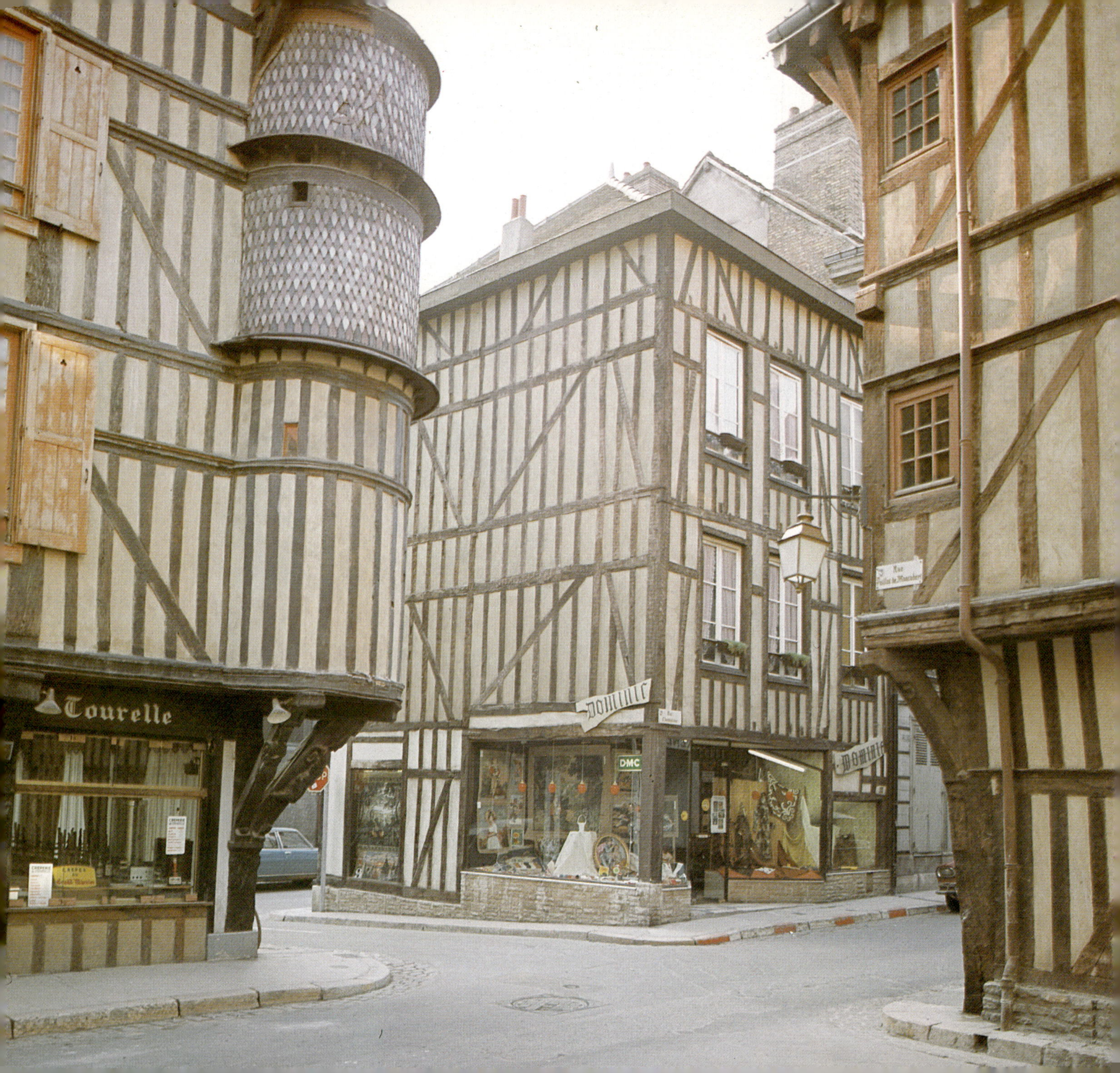
Tourelle
DMC

Troyes is the first big town on the Seine.
This is how it looked about 100 years ago.
In the Middle Ages it was the capital of Champagne.
Many markets, fairs and **jousts** were held here.

This is how the old part of Troyes looks today.
You can see that the streets are still narrow.

On the Outskirts of Paris

Below Troyes the Seine flows through flat country.
Along the banks there are straight lines of poplar trees.
The artist Monet painted this picture of the countryside.
➡

At Romilly the River Aube joins
the Seine.
The river is deeper and wider.
Small barges work on the river.
They carry cargoes to and from
Paris.
At this point the Seine is
145 km (90 miles) from its source.

This is one of the large barges which works on the Seine. As the river gets near Paris, there is more river traffic. The barges pass many more houses and factories. There are also big power stations and **fuel depots**. In between the new houses and factories there are farms and roads lined with poplar trees.

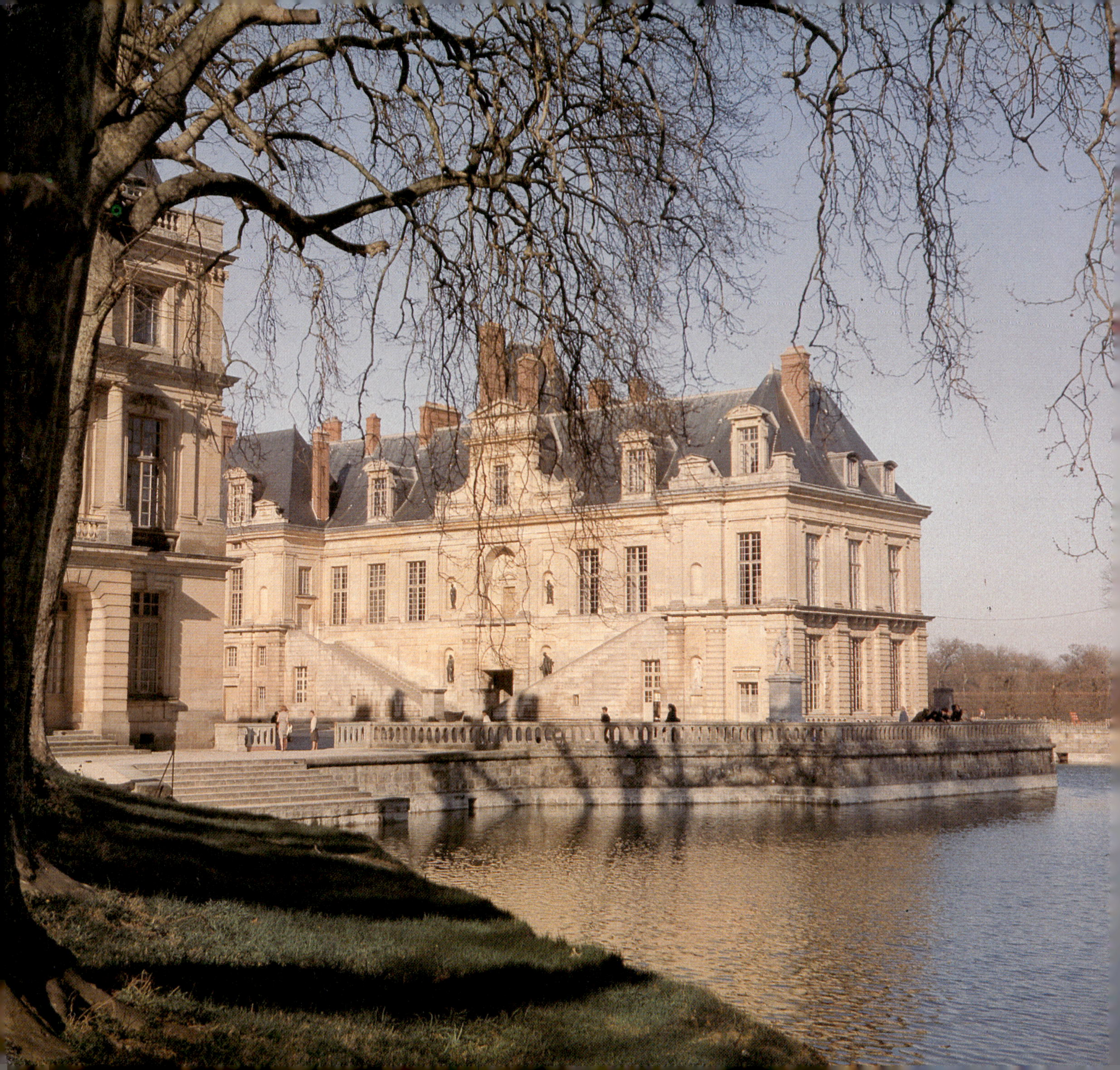

▲ This is the River Seine as it gets close to Paris.

◀ Here is the Palace of Fontainebleau near Paris.
It once belonged to the kings of France.

The Seine in Paris

Over 8 million people live in Paris.
It is the meeting point of all the main roads
and railways in France.
This picture shows Paris and the Seine in winter.

When the Seine reaches Paris
it divides into two arms.
Between them are two islands
on which the city first grew.
You can see how many bridges
have been built across the Seine.

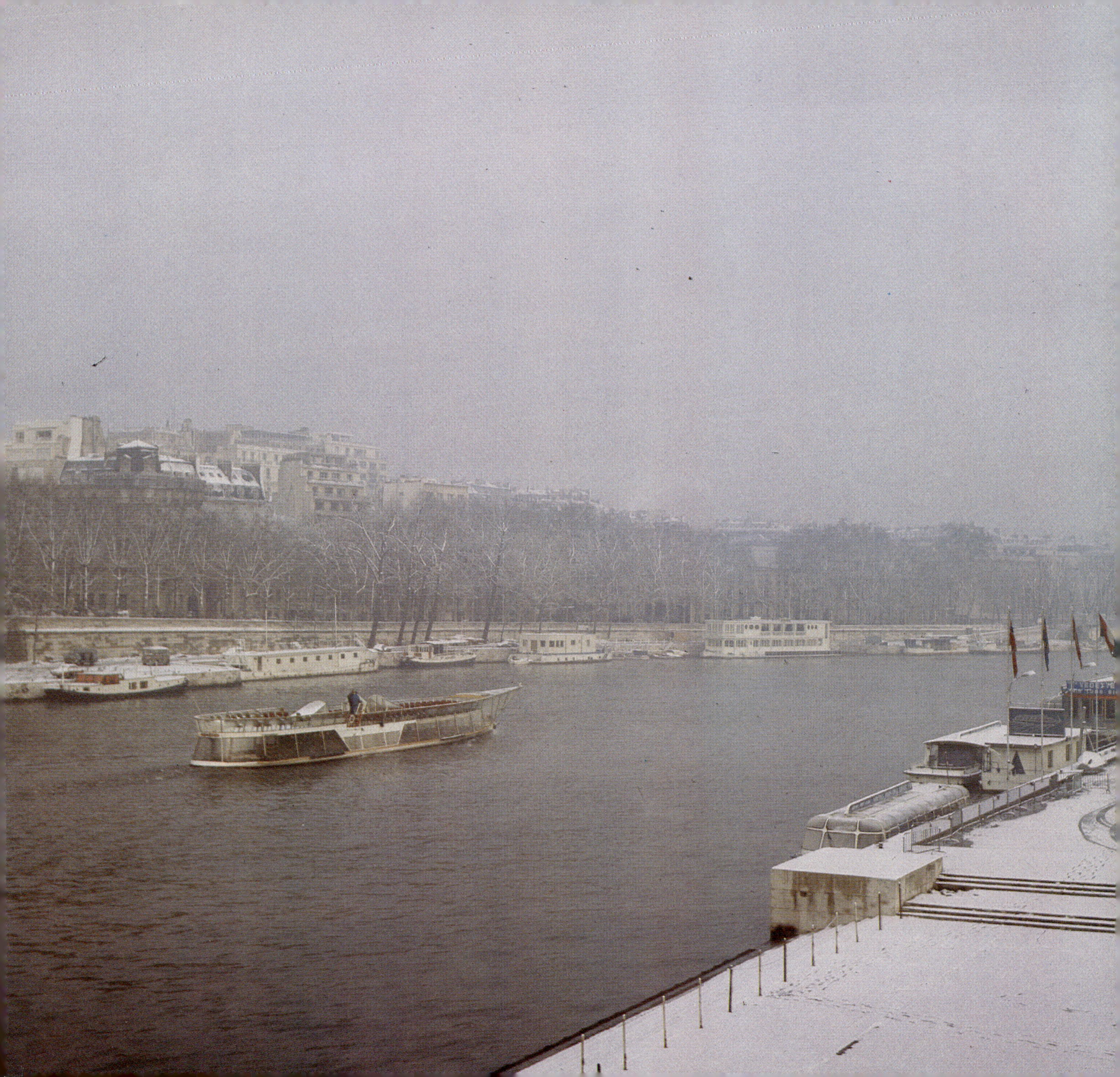

Here is a picture of Paris about 200 years ago.
How can you tell that the Seine was important even then?
What different things are people doing on the banks?

Tourists love the Seine in Paris.
Along the riverside is a wide
pavement shaded by trees.
Books and prints are sold
from green huts.
Artists sketch and paint the
famous sights.

Below the **embankment** there is
another path on the river's edge.
Fishermen sit here away from
the crowds.
The famous 'arches of Paris' can
be seen from here.
Beggars called *clochards* live
under some of the arches.

Here is one of the most
decorated bridges in Paris.
It is Alexander III bridge.

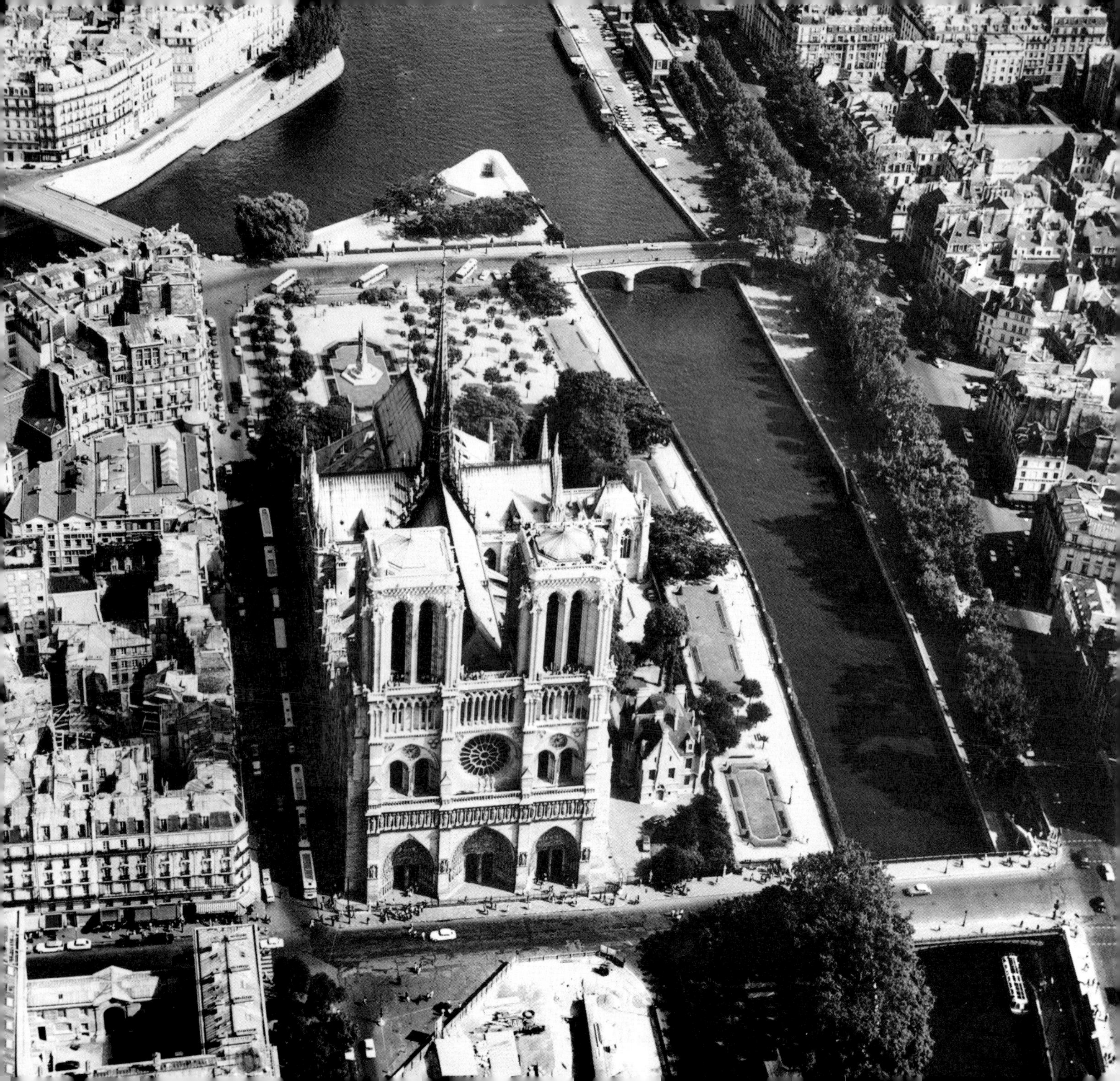

Here is part of the embankment.
It is a quiet place where
people can talk and paint.

In the 1960s an **expressway**
was built along one river bank.
The traffic destroyed the peace
and quiet.
The public stopped the other
bank being used the same way.

This is a view from the air of
Notre Dame cathedral.
Other famous historic buildings
share the same island.
One is the Conciergerie.
It was an ancient fortress.
Nobles were put in prison
here in the French Revolution.

Do you like this painting of the Royal Bridge?

Here is the Conciergerie floodlit at night.
It does not look grim but it was the place where the last Queen of France was held before she was executed in 1793.

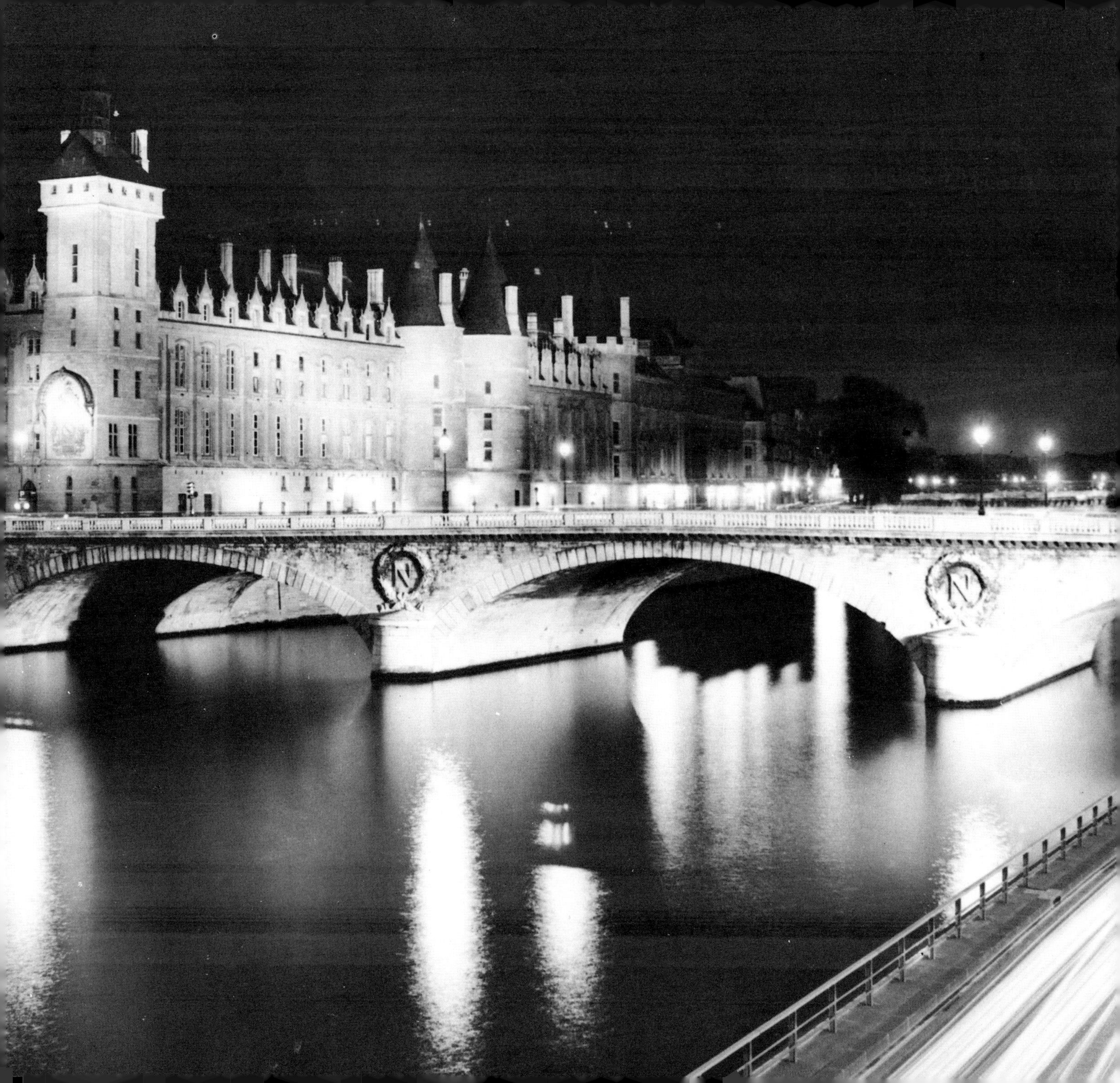

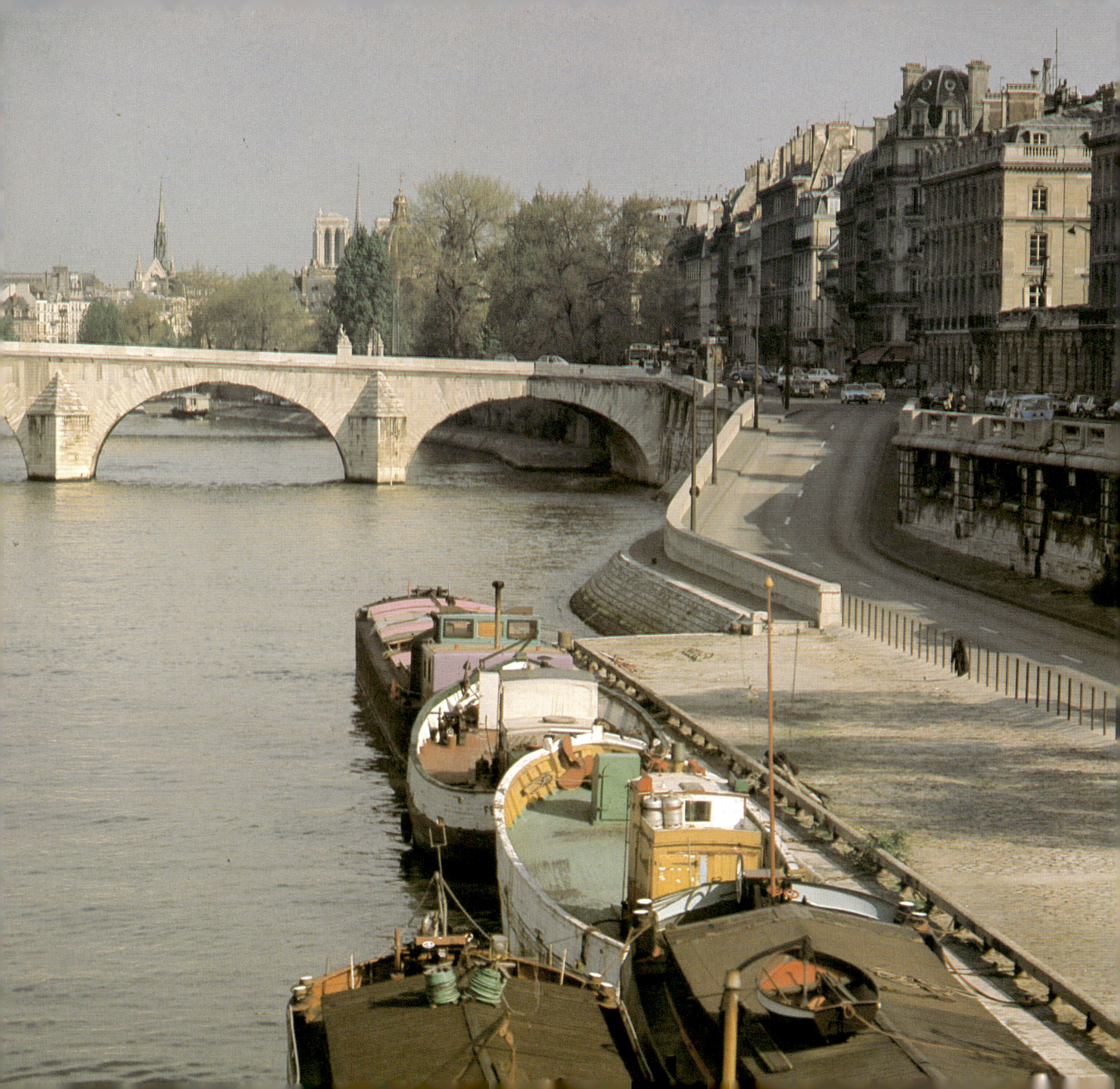

The Seine divides Paris into
two parts.
They are called the **right bank**
and the **left bank.**
Most of the shopping streets are
on the right bank.
The University of Paris is on
the left bank.
The student area is called the
Latin Quarter.

The Louvre is on the right bank.
It is the largest palace in
the world.
Now it is a famous museum and
art gallery.

Even in the city centre working
barges can be seen.
The fishermen seem to take
little notice of them.

Here is one of the bookstalls on the embankment.

Do you know this world famous landmark?
It is the church of Sacré Coeur in Montmartre.

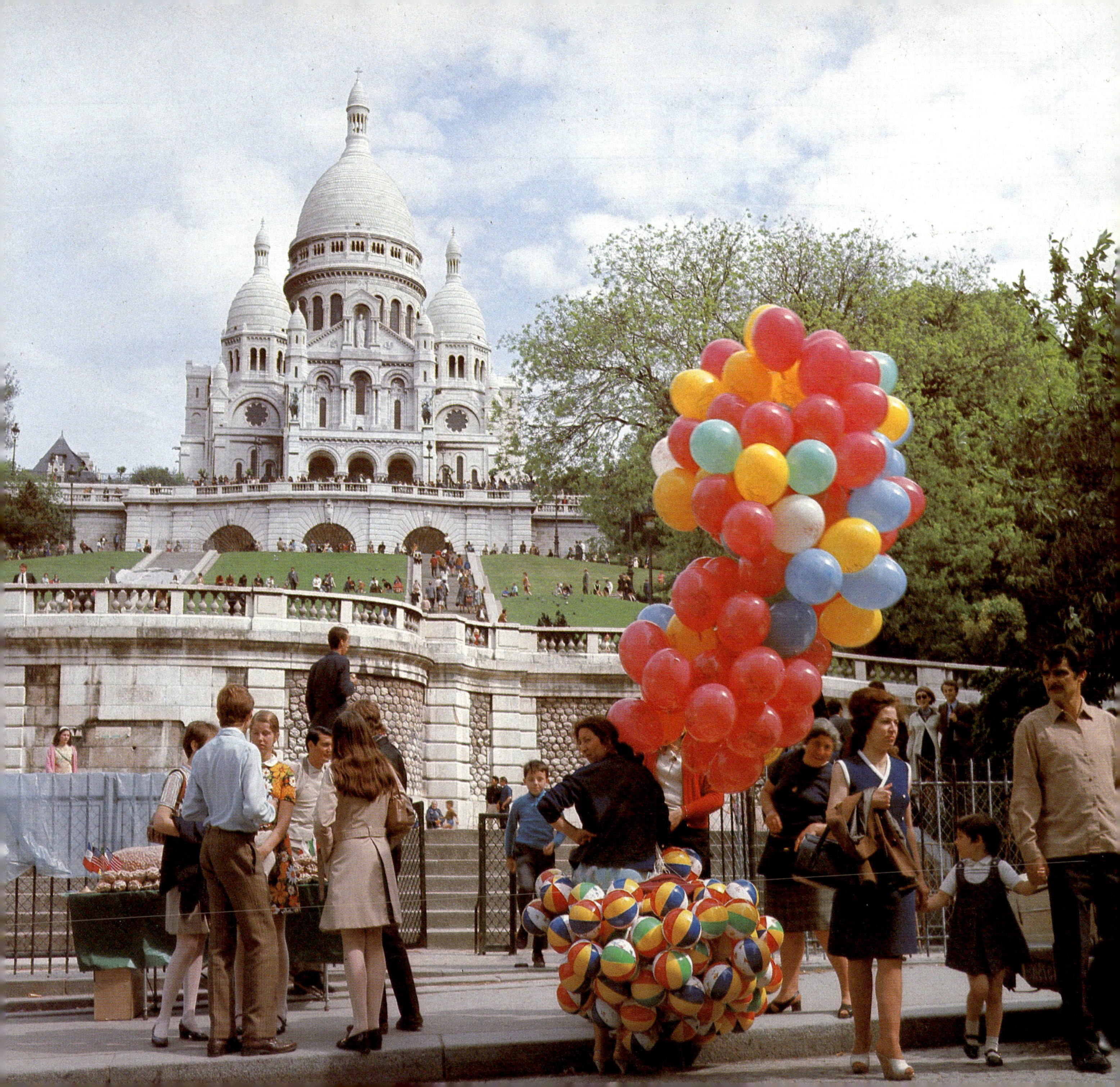

The Suburbs of Paris

The central province of France is the Île de France.
Paris has spread outwards into the countryside.
Some places in the Île de France are rich, others are poor.

This is the industrial **suburb** called Grenelle.
Along the river are small factories and warehouses.
Many are now disused.
There are rubbish tips which **pollute** the river too.

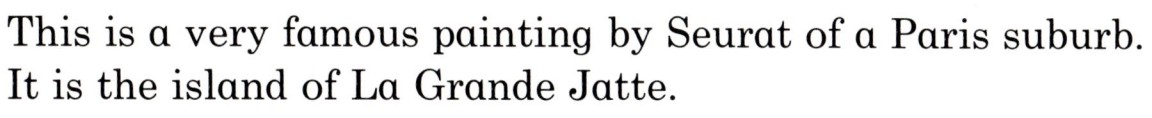

This is a very famous painting by Seurat of a Paris suburb.
It is the island of La Grande Jatte.
It shows people enjoying themselves on a Sunday afternoon.

Industrial suburbs have grown around ancient centres.
Kings and queens are buried in this church at St Denis.
St Denis is now a busy industrial suburb.

This **château** is on a hill above the Seine.
In the French Revolution it was used as a refuge for
noble families who fled here from Paris.

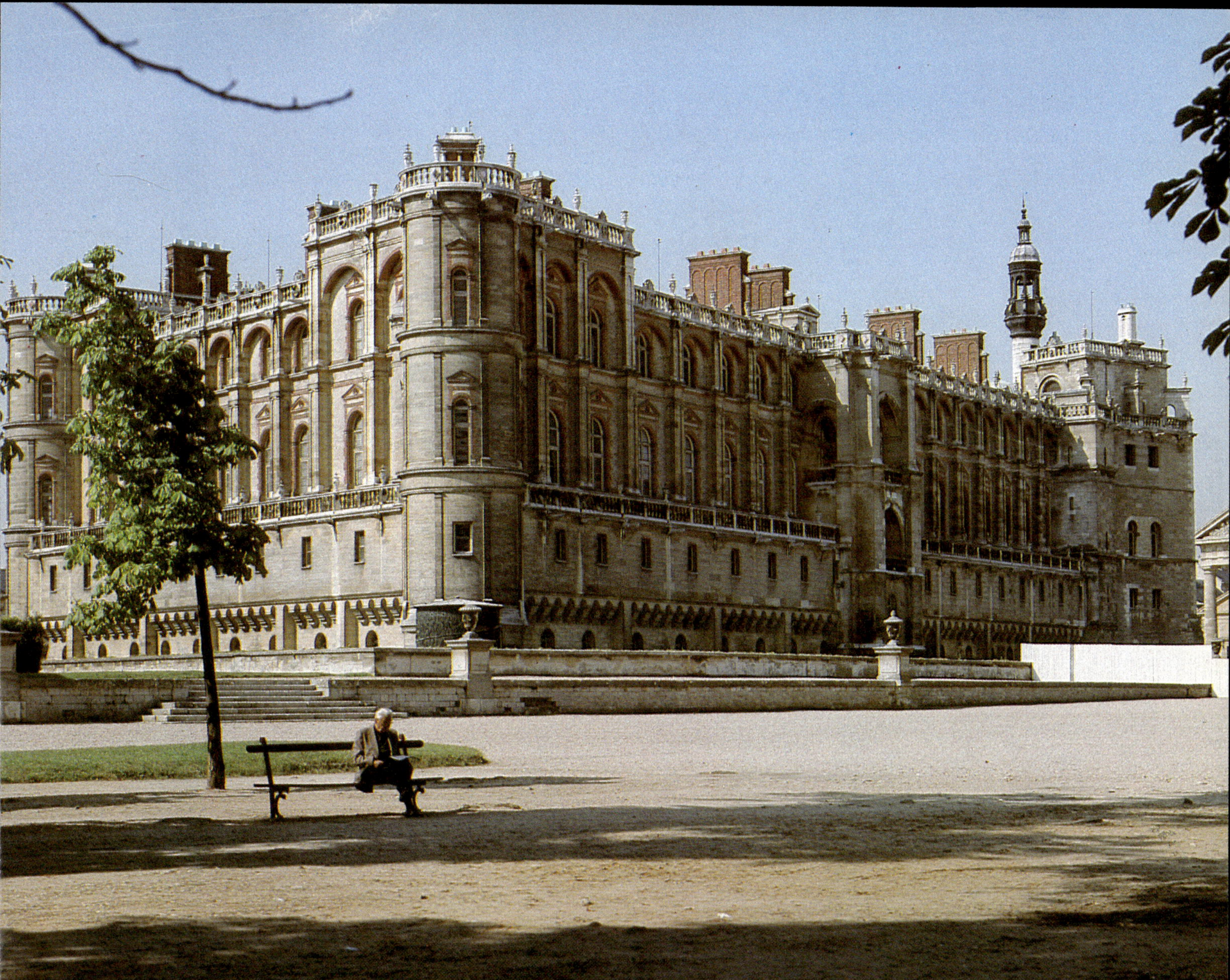

This is Conflans.
It is a busy barge depot.
Barges load and refuel here.
From Paris to the sea there is
a great deal of traffic.
Barges carry over 40 million
tonnes of cargo a year.

Retired **bargees** live in house-
boats along the river bank.
One of these barges has been
turned into a church.
Can you see a decorated barge
near the church?

Here is the St Martin canal.
It was built to take some of
the heavy traffic off the Seine.

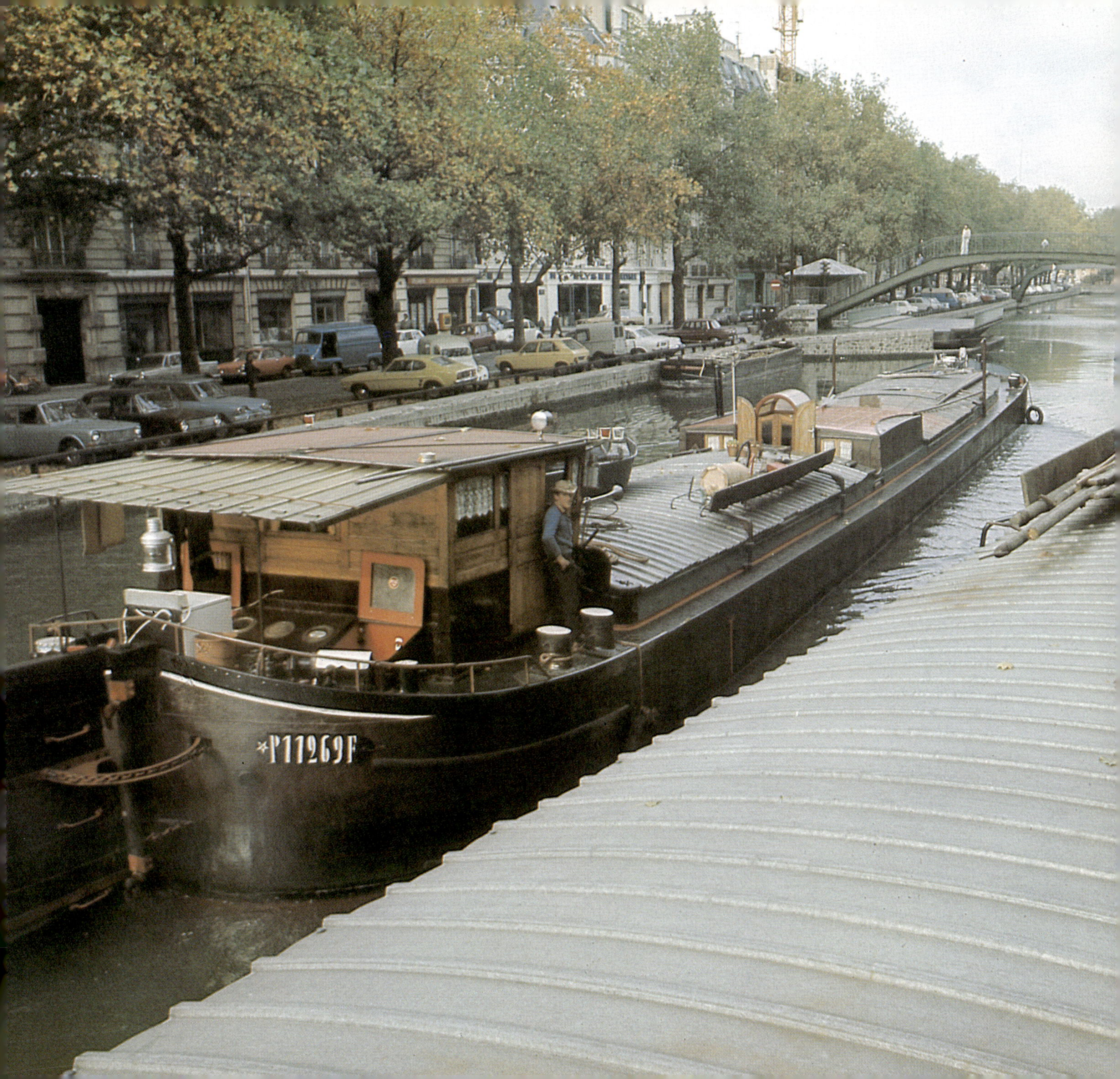
P11269F

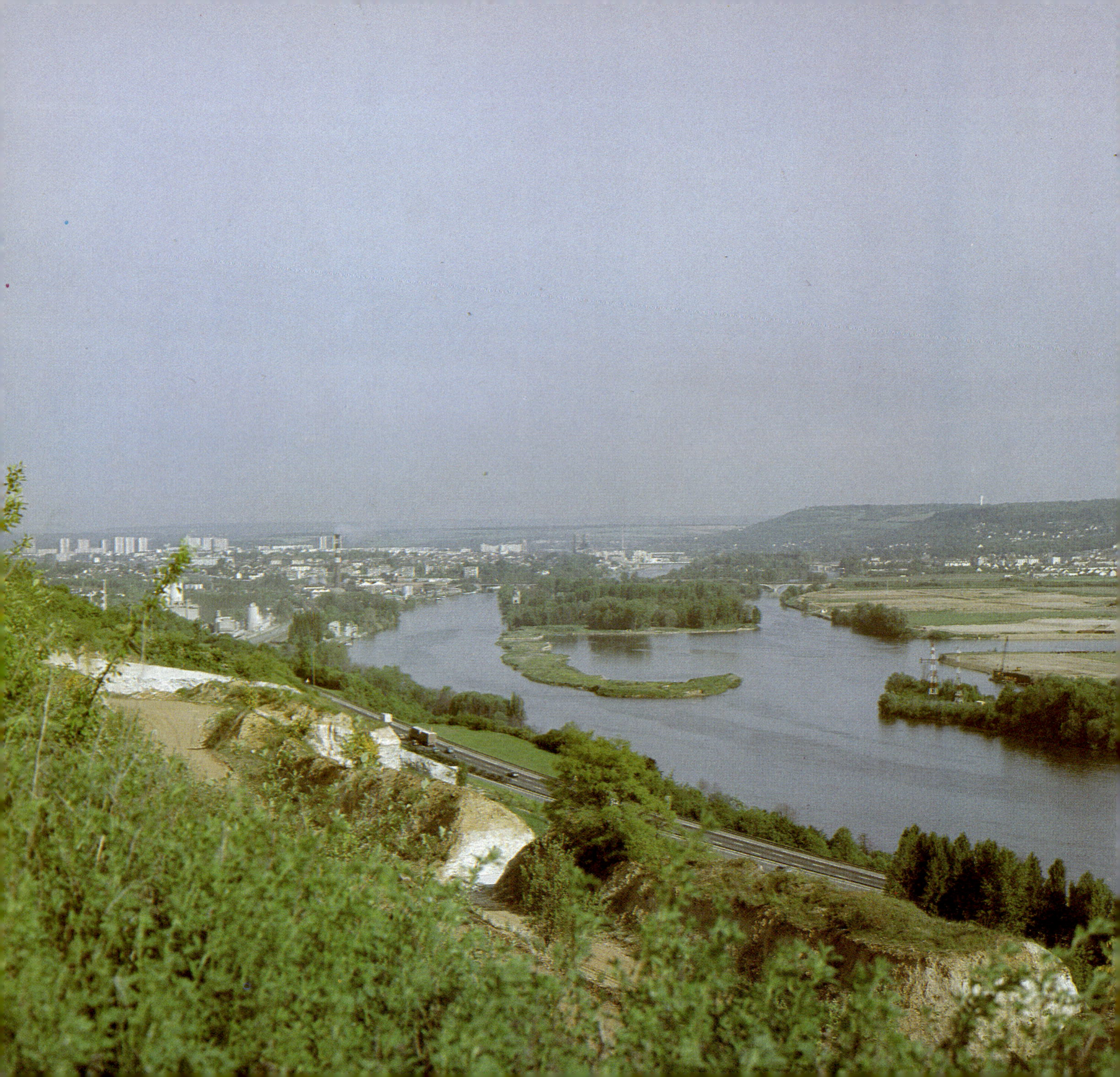

This is the River Seine near the town of Mantes.
Between Paris and Rouen the Seine flows through wooded farmland like this.

The Seine has many **tributaries** which also carry barge traffic. At Conflans the Seine is joined by the River Oise.
This barge has moored near a riverside restaurant.

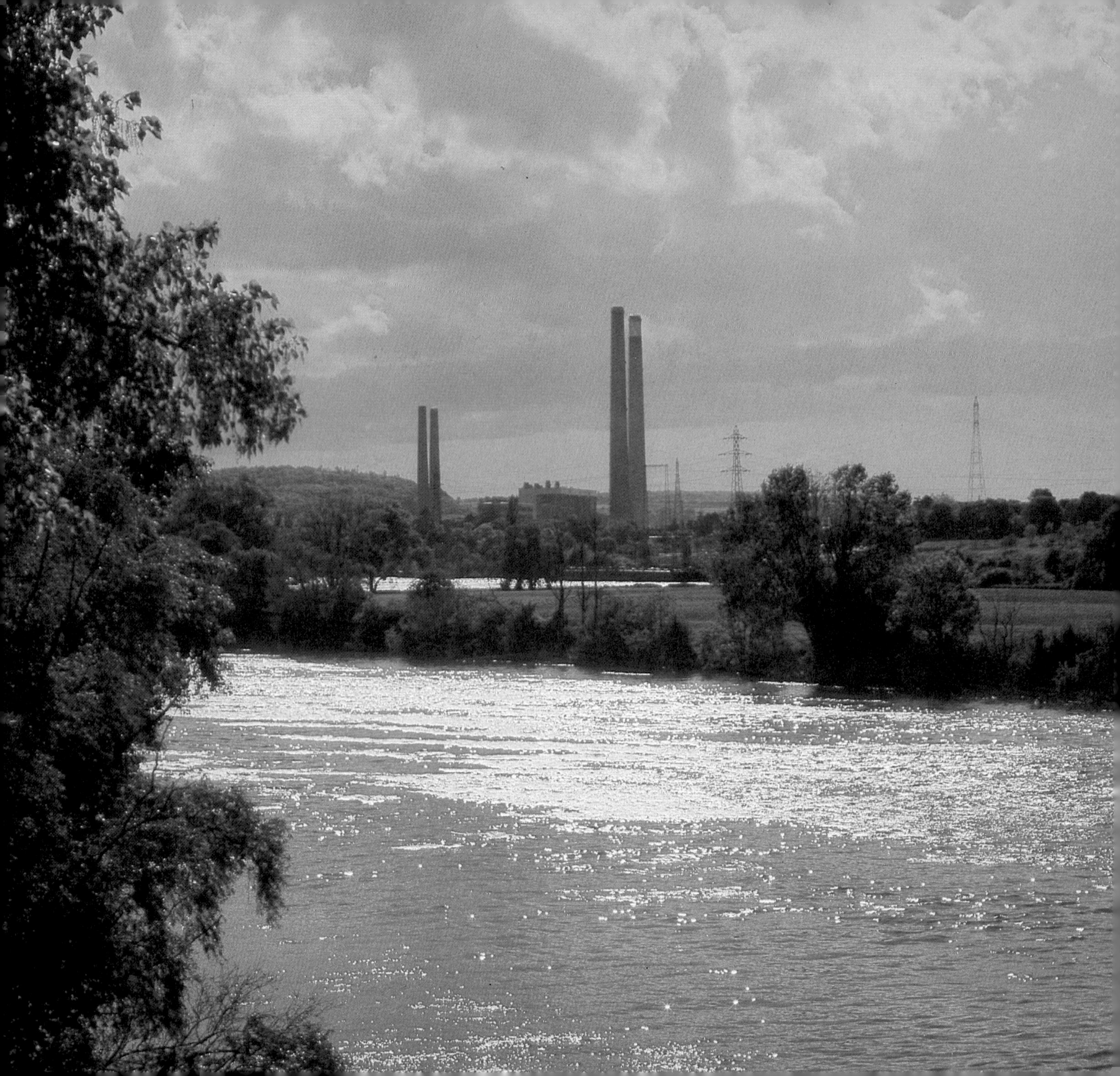

One of the main industries along the river is oil refining. This refinery is near Mantes. Industry pollutes the Seine. At Mantes there is oil and scum on the water.
Cement factories and quarries also pour waste into the Seine so there are not many fish. Clothes can no longer be washed in the river water.

The village of Giverny lies where the Epte joins the Seine. It is famous because the artist Monet lived there. Above is his painting of a water-lily pond.
Below is the point where the two rivers meet.

The Seine in Normandy

The Seine now enters the province of Normandy.
This was the home of the Vikings (**Normans**).
William the Conqueror was Duke of Normandy in 1066.
Here there are gentle hills with patches of bare chalk.
You can see the white chalk cliffs above the
lovely village of Les Andelys in this picture.

Normandy is very beautiful.
The villages along the river
are pretty with many trees.
Here are the remains of an old
bridge at the village of Vernon.

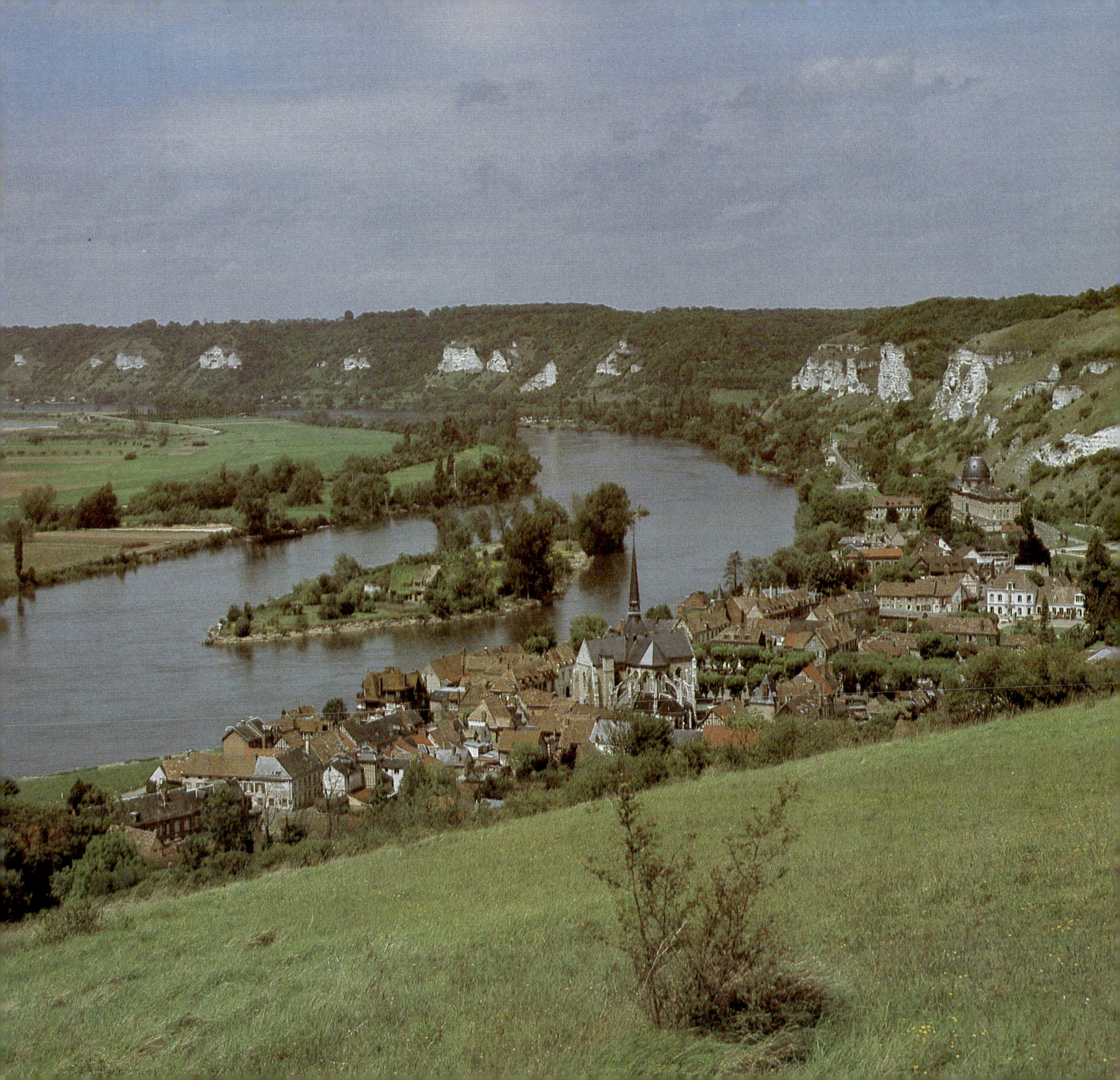

Here is an old house in Vernon.
It has been carefully restored.

This is Château Gaillard.
It means 'swaggering castle'.
It was built on a cliff by
the river.

The castle was built by
Richard the Lionheart.
He wanted to build a castle
which no one could capture.
It was the greatest fort
in Europe.
But in 1204 the King of France
took it from King John of
England.
Later King Louis X of France
had his queen murdered here.

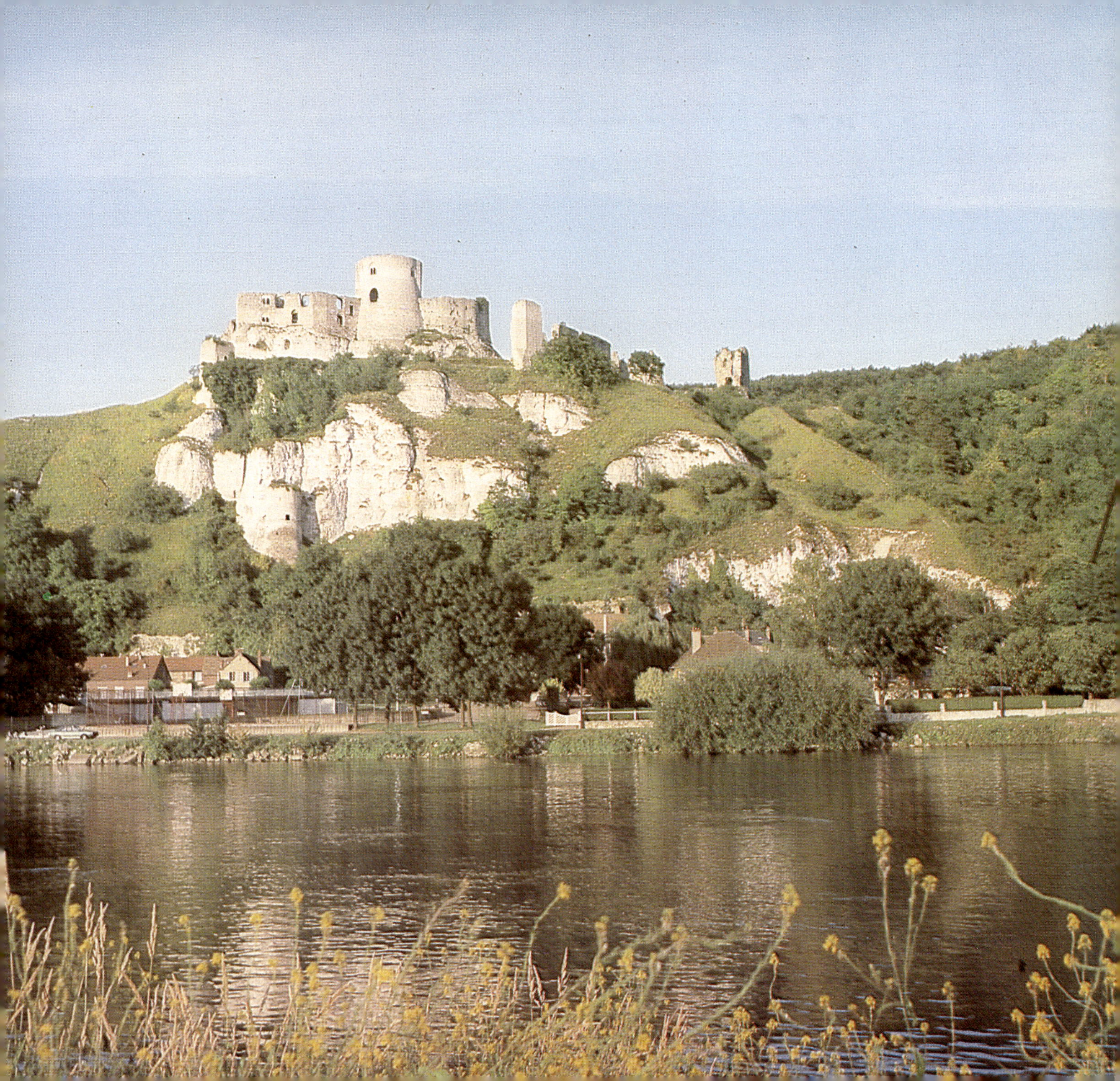

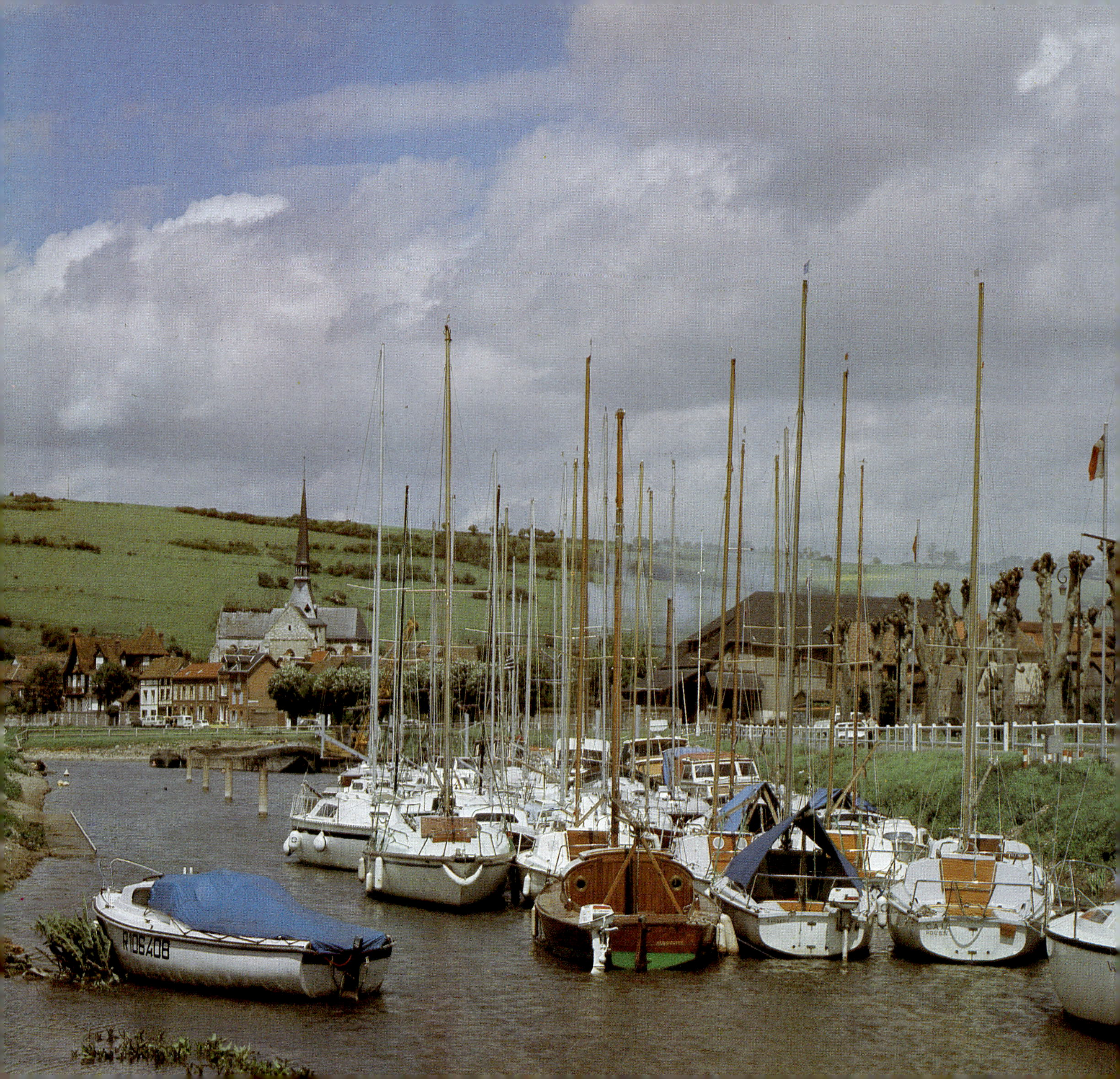
R106408

People use the Seine for fun.
These are private yachts.
They are moored near a village.
Tourists go to Normandy for summer holidays.
They enjoy visiting ancient castles and churches.
There are also many beautiful villages and towns.

This hill is called the Hill of the Two Lovers.
A cruel knight called Rulph had a daughter named Calixte.
She fell in love with a poor man but could not marry him.
One day she was attacked by a wild boar.
The poor man saved her and asked to marry her.
Her father said he could marry her if he could carry Calixte to the top of the hill without stopping.
He did it but died of a heart attack.
Calixte then killed herself.

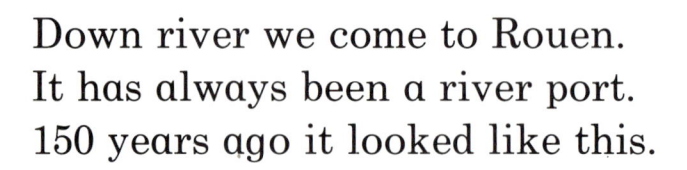

Down river we come to Rouen.
It has always been a river port.
150 years ago it looked like this.

Here is an aerial view of the modern city.

Rouen has many old buildings.

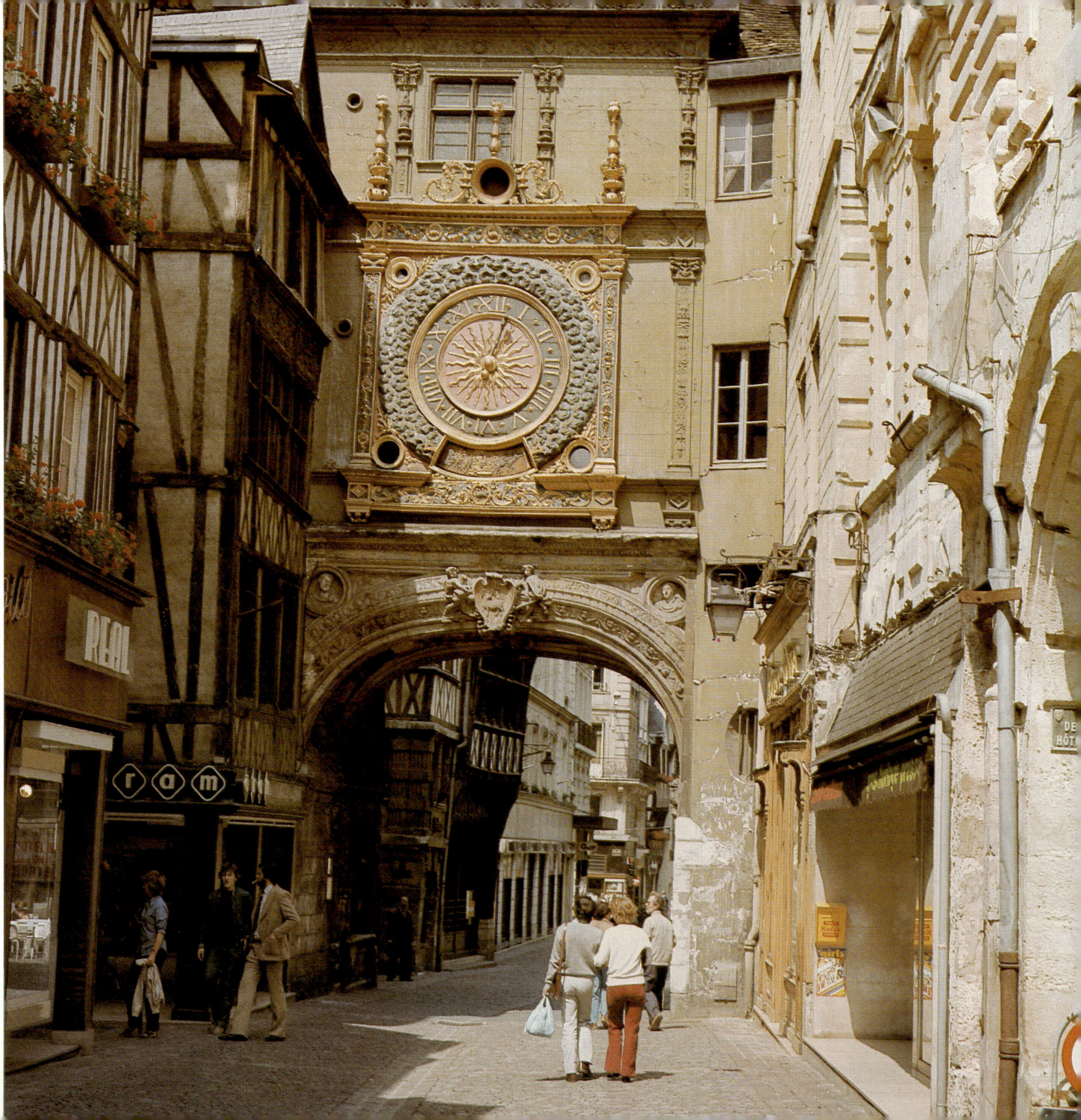
REAL
ram

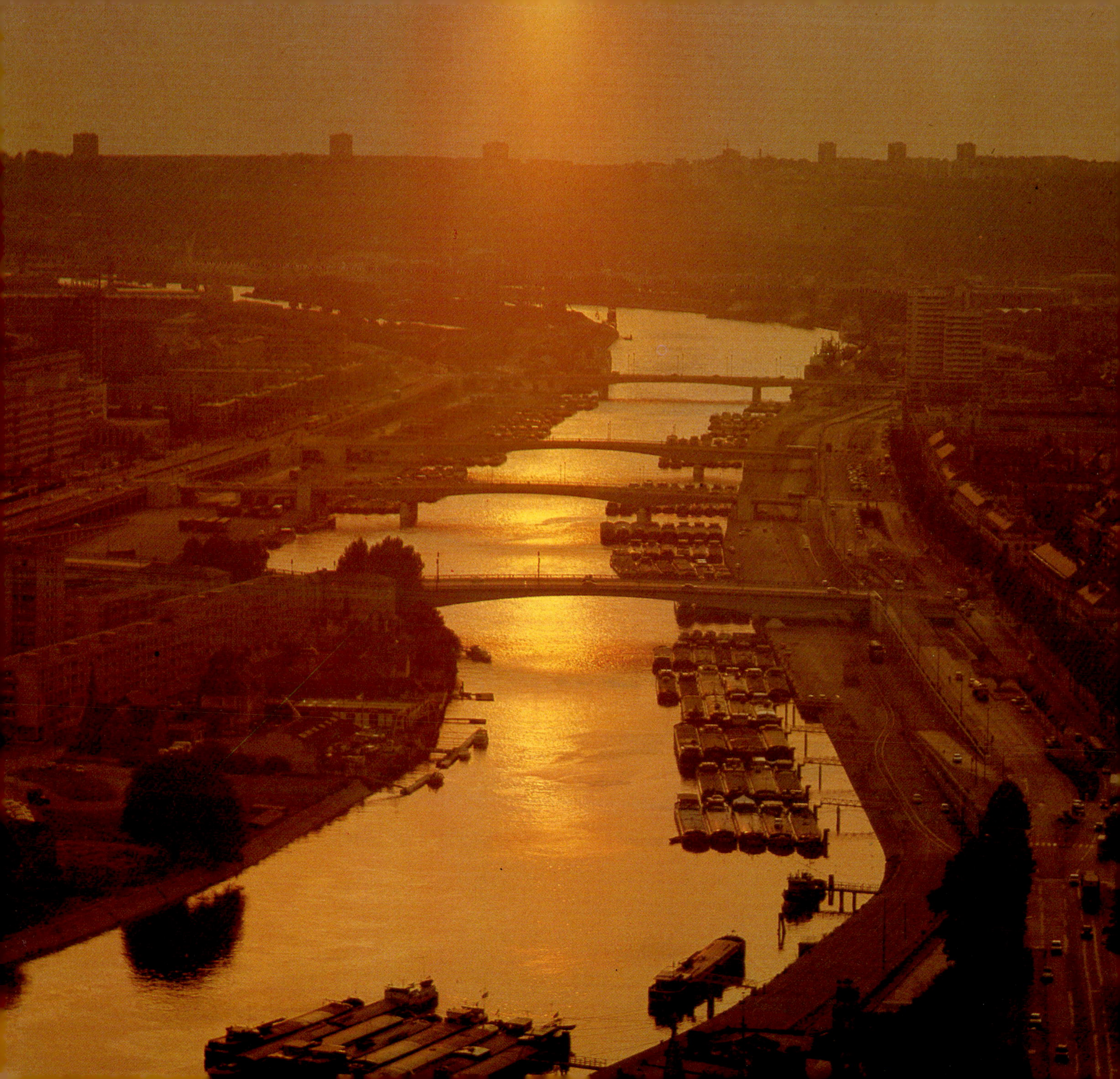

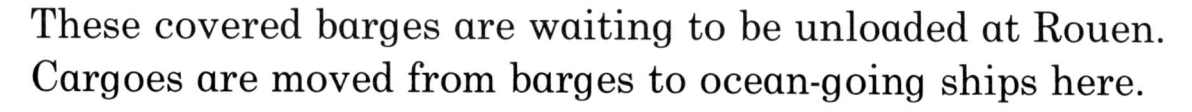

These covered barges are waiting to be unloaded at Rouen. Cargoes are moved from barges to ocean-going ships here.

This is a picture of the port of Rouen at sunset.

Rouen was famous in history.
Joan of Arc was burned here.
She led the French into battle
against the English but
the English captured her.
She was convicted of witchcraft
and burned to death in 1431.

◀ This modern church is in Rouen.
It is a memorial to Joan of Arc.

These are the ruins of a beautiful abbey near Rouen.
Many old buildings were destroyed in the Second World War.
In 1940 German invaders burned down most of the old part. ▶
In 1944 all the bridges were burned when the Allies
attacked the Germans to free Rouen.

Below Rouen the river **currents** get stronger and wilder.
There are many **sandbanks** so it is difficult to navigate boats.

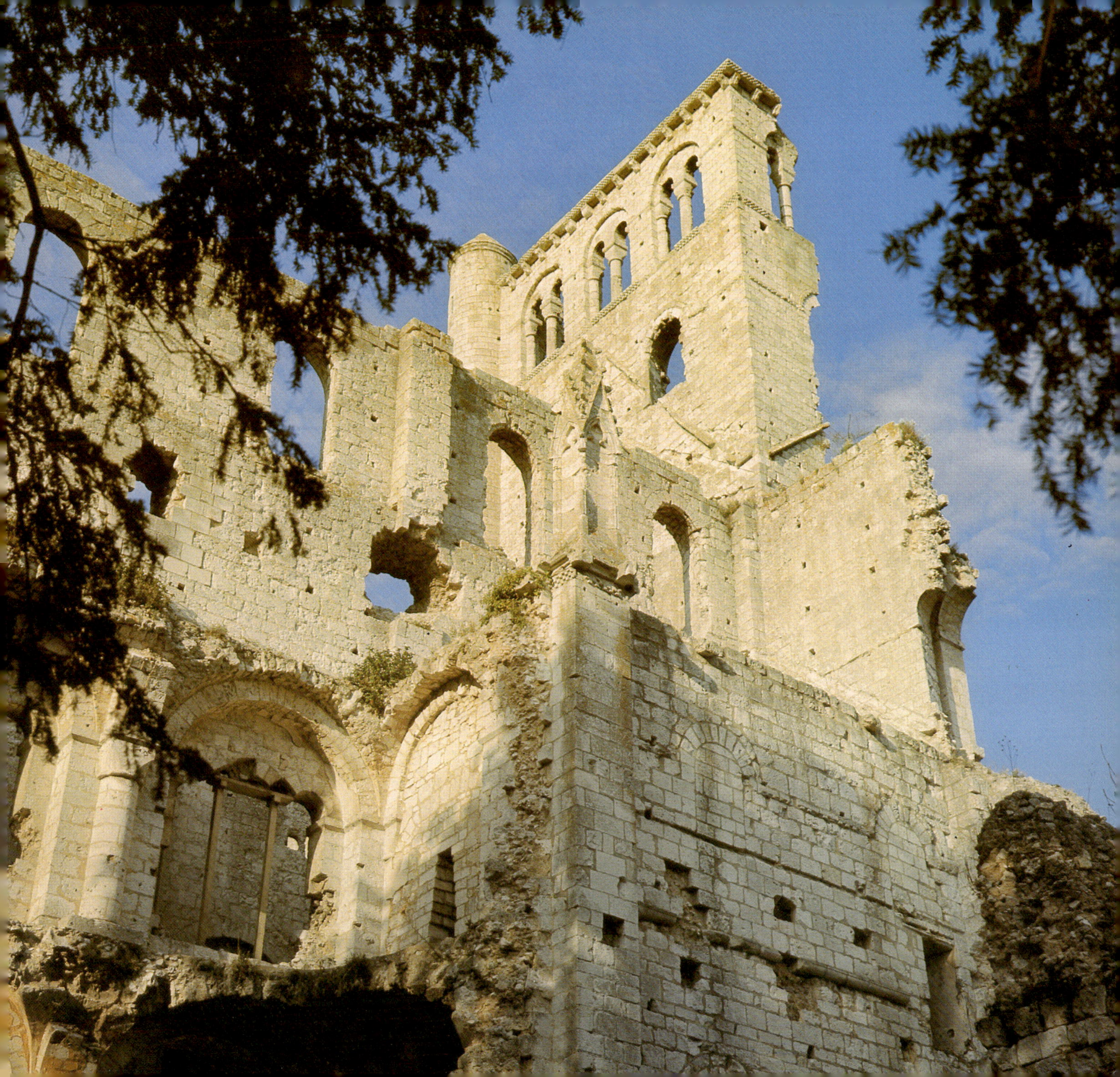

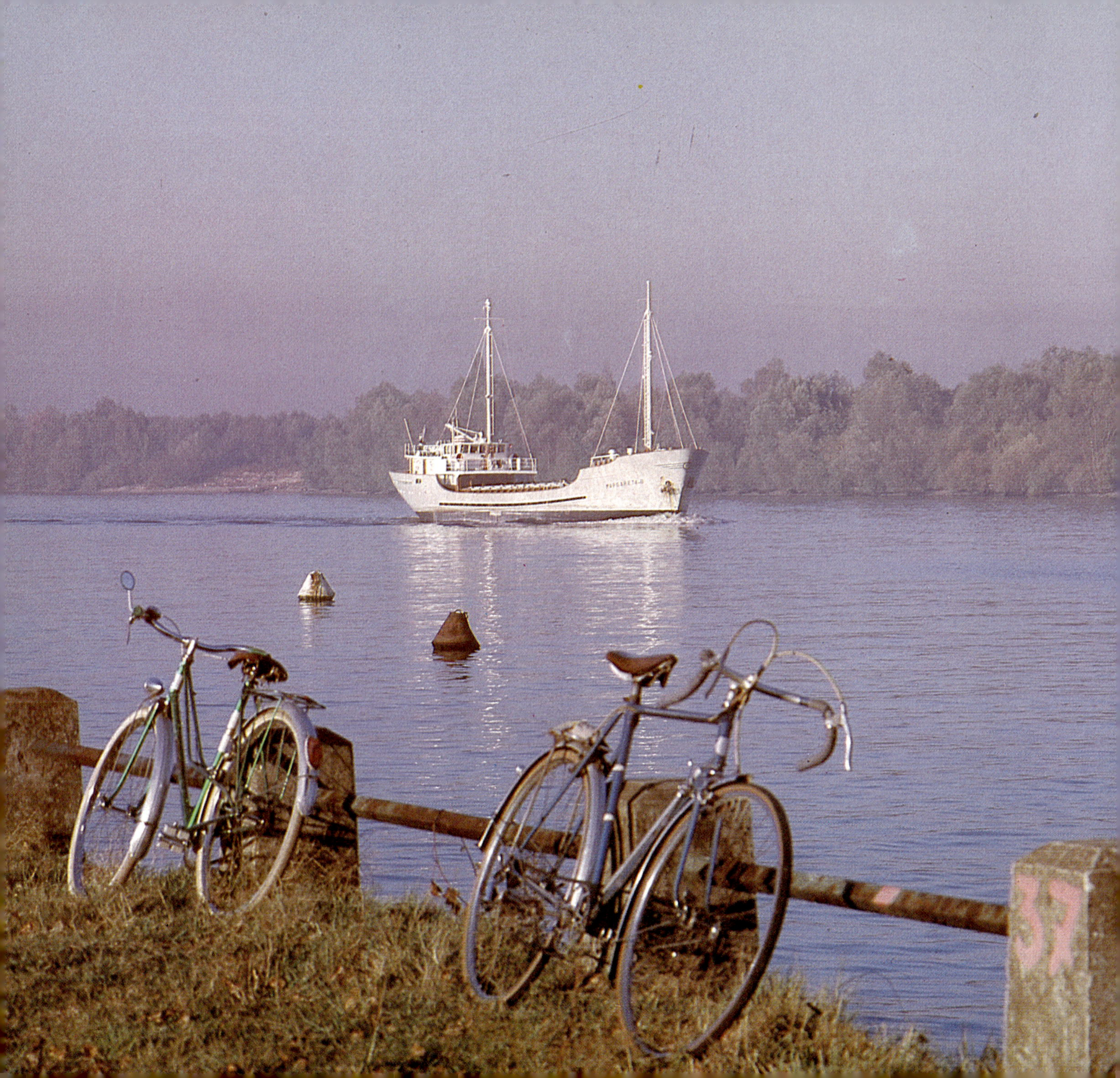

If you stand on the Hill of the Two Lovers you can look towards the **estuary** of the River Seine.
This is the view you will see.
Much of the land is very flat and marshy.

This large ship is sailing between Rouen and the sea.

The Seine Estuary

This is the Tancarville suspension bridge across the Seine estuary.
It stretches 1,400 metres (4,593 feet) and
is one of the longest bridges in Europe.

As the Seine reaches the sea
it becomes wider.
It is no longer a calm river
and the waters are rough.
Near its mouth the Seine is
very polluted and crowded.
Here is the huge oil refinery
at Port Jerome.

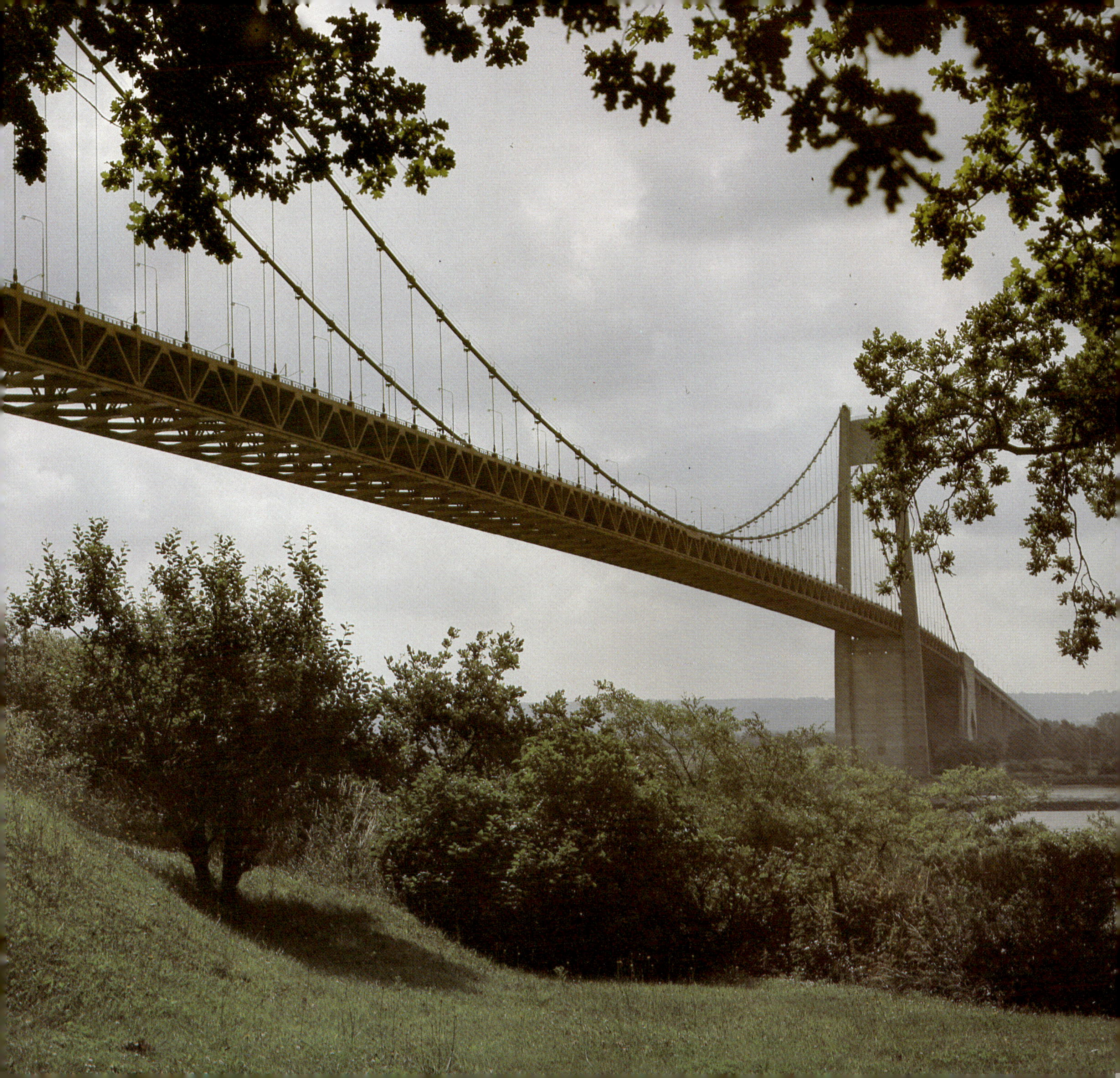

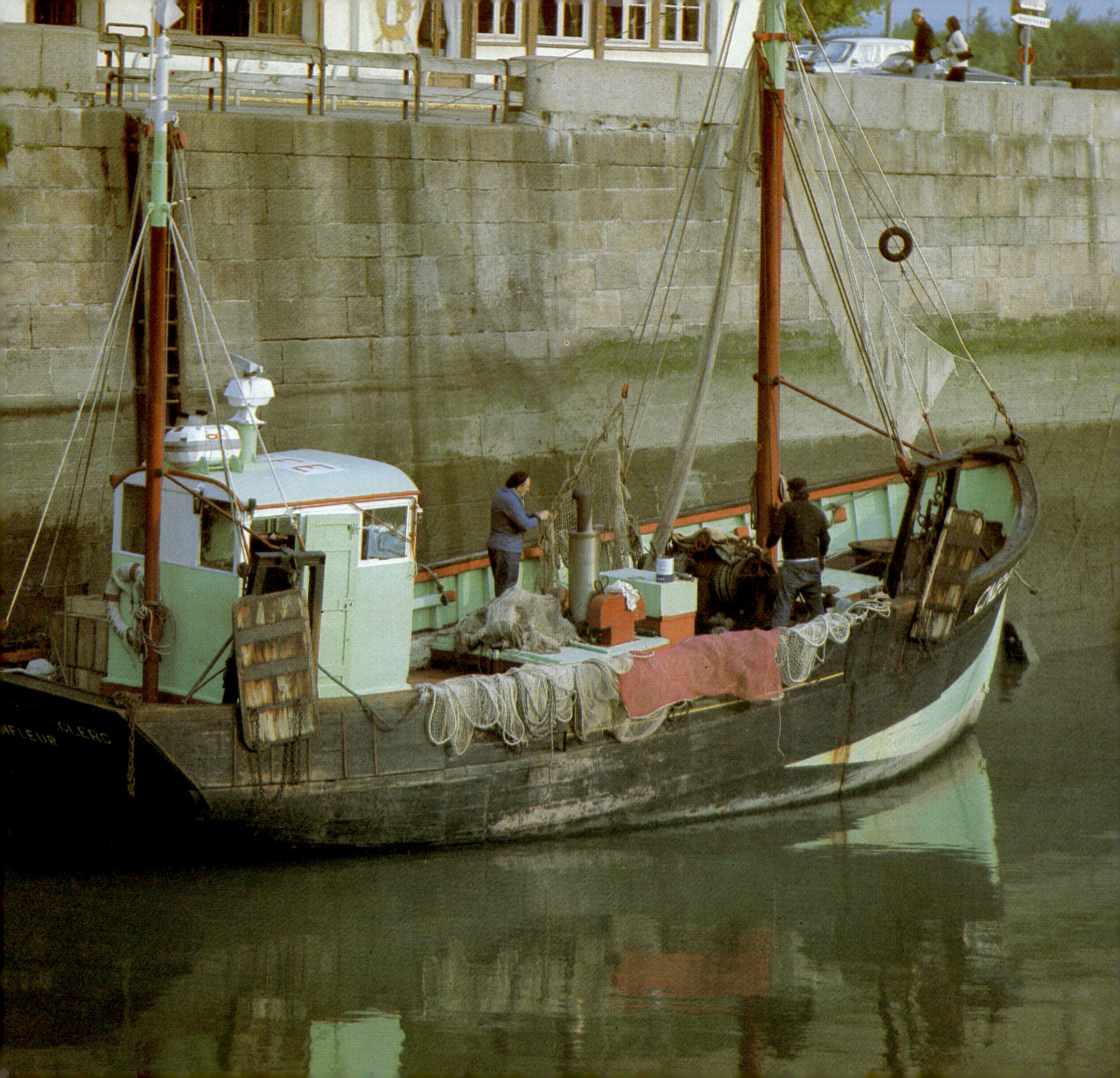
NFLEUR
CLERC

Most of the estuary is flat marshland.
There are many factories in this area.
This is a typical scene near the mouth of the Seine.

There is much fishing on the coast of Normandy.
This boat is in the ancient port of Honfleur.
It was once the chief port on the Seine.

This picture shows Le Havre about 150 years ago.
It was very busy then.

Here is the port today.
It was almost completely rebuilt after the Second World War.

This is a scene in the port of Le Havre.
Le Havre is now the chief port on the Seine.
It is also the chief port of France.
It handles trade from North and South America as well as Africa.

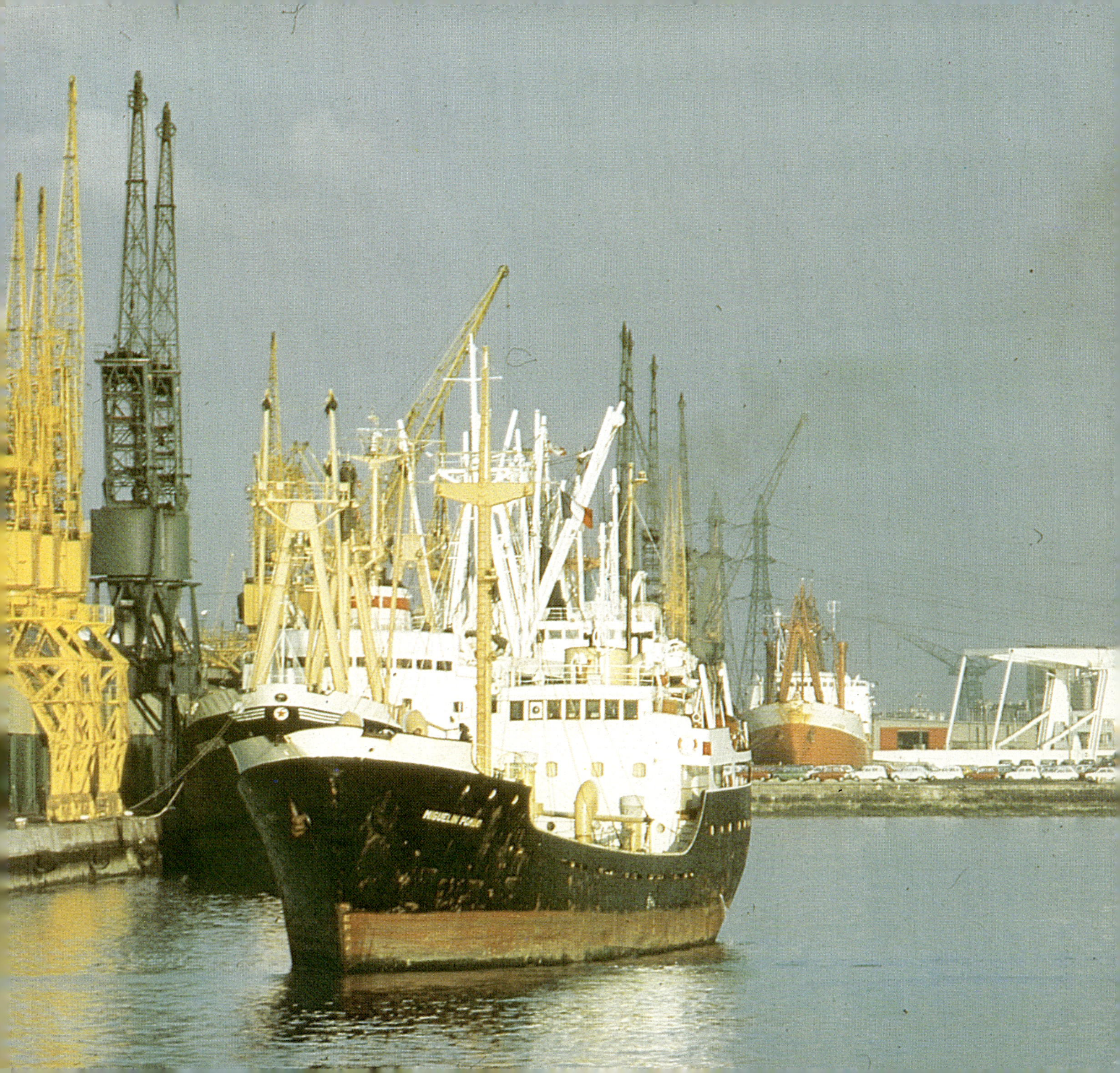

Glossary

Barge A flat-bottomed boat used for carrying cargo on rivers.

Bargee A person who works on a barge.

Château A castle, country house or mansion. France is well known for its châteaux.

Current Water in the river or sea which flows in a particular direction.

Embankment A natural or artificial barrier along a river bank to protect the land from flooding.

Estuary The wide part of the river leading to the sea.

Expressway A fast modern road like a motorway.

Fuel depots Places where fuels such as coal and oil are unloaded and stored.

Joust Fight between two knights on horses using lances.

Left Bank The artistic and university quarter of Paris.

Normans Viking invaders (northmen or norsemen) who raided France and later settled around the mouth of the Seine.

Pollute To poison rivers, seas or land by depositing rubbish, oil or dangerous chemicals from industry.

Province One of the regions into which France is divided; example, Burgundy is a province.

Right Bank The business and public building area of central Paris.

Sandbank An underwater bank of sand in the sea or a river. It may be exposed at low tide or when the river is low.

Source The point at which a river begins.

Suburbs Residential areas on the edges of towns and cities.

Suspension bridge A bridge which is hung across a river on wire or chain cables fixed to towers.

Tributary A stream or river which flows into a larger one.

Index

Alexander III bridge   25
arches of Paris   25
artists   10, 25, 41

Burgundy   12, 15

Champagne   15
Château Gaillard   46
Châtillon   13, 14, 15
Conciergerie   27, 28
Conflans   38, 41

estuary   57, 58, 61

Fontainebleau   21
French Revolution   27, 36

Giverny   41
Grenelle   34

Honfleur   61

Île de France   34

Joan of Arc   54

Latin Quarter   31
Left Bank   27, 31
Les Andelys   44
Le Havre   62, 63
Louis X   46
Louvre, the   31

Mantes   41, 143
Monet   18, 41
Montmartre   31

Normandy   44, 49, 61
Notre Dame   8, 27

Oise, river   41

Paris   8, 10, 11, 19, 21, 22, 24, 25, 31, 34, 36, 38, 41
Port Jerome   58

Richard the Lionheart   46
Right Bank   31
Rouen   41, 49, 50, 53
Royal bridge (Pont Royal)   28

St Denis   36
St Martin canal   38
Sacré Coeur   31
Second World War   14, 54, 63

Tancarville bridge   58
Troyes   17, 18

Vikings   44

William the Conqueror   44

Picture acknowledgements

The illustrations in this book were supplied by: J. Allan Cash *frontispiece*, 9, 11, 13, 14, 16, 23, 60; Collection of the Art Institute of Chicago 35; Camerapix Hutchison Library 12, 15; Colour Library International 25 *bottom*, 30, 31 *top*; James Davis 29; Documentation Française, Paris 21, 22, 25 *top*, 26, 32, 50 *bottom*, 58, 62, 63; Mary Evans Picture Library 28; C. Gibb 8, 31 *bottom*, 44, 47; National Gallery, London 10, 18, 43; Mansell Collection 17, 24, 36, 49, 50 *top*, 62; Topham Picture Library 19, 20, 27, 33, 39, 46, 55, 56; T. A. Wilkie 37, 38 *both*, 40, 41, 42, 43, 45, 48, 51, 53, 54, 57, 59, 61; Zefa *front cover*. Artwork by Alan Gunston.

ENGLISH CHANNEL

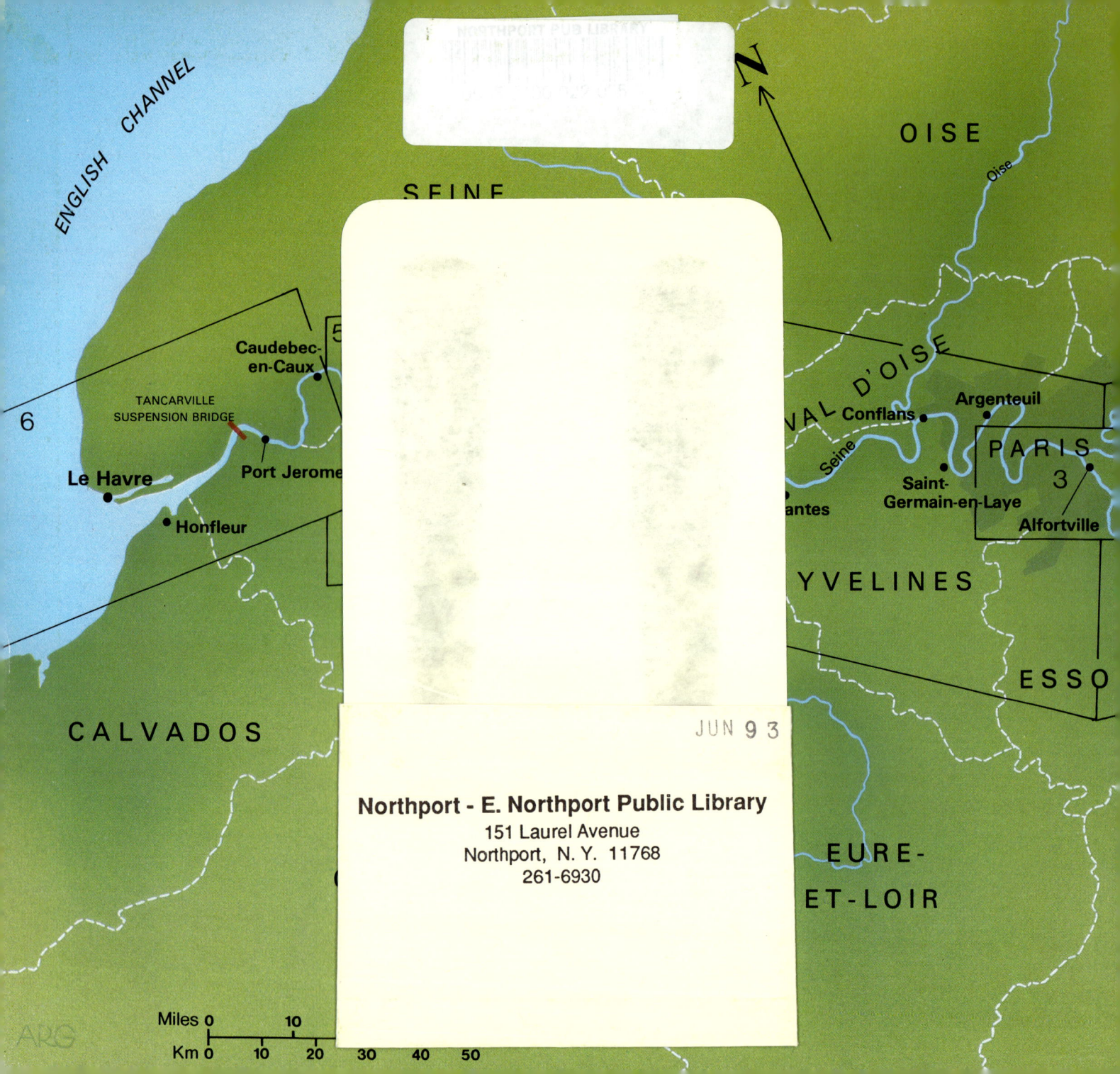

OISE

SEINE

N

VAL D'OISE

Caudebec-en-Caux

TANCARVILLE SUSPENSION BRIDGE

Argenteuil

Conflans

Le Havre

Port Jerome

PARIS

Saint-Germain-en-Laye

Alfortville

Honfleur

YVELINES

ESSO

CALVADOS

JUN 9 3

Northport - E. Northport Public Library
151 Laurel Avenue
Northport, N. Y. 11768
261-6930

EURE-ET-LOIR

ARG

Miles 0   10
Km 0   10   20   30   40   50